T0374022

Sara the Famous

Written and Illustrated by
Lisa Jean Collins

To order additional copies of this book, contact:
Xlibris
1-888-795-4274
www.Xlibris.com
Orders@Xlibris.com

ISBN: Softcover   978-1-4257-0640-1

Library of Congress Control Number: 2006900172

Print information available on the last page

Rev. date: 11/20/2019

For Sara,
Based on a true story.

Hi! My name is Sara, and I would like to tell you about my life. My life has not always been easy. Sometimes I have been teased at school because of the way I look or the way I talk. Sometimes even teachers would be mean to me and take special things away from me. Sometimes I would imagine that things were different about my life. I would pretend to be someone else, or I would make up stories about my life and people would think they were true. But even during the tough times, I always felt in my heart that things were going to be okay. That's because my mom and dad love me very much. And do you know who else loves me? It's Jesus. Someday I'm going to be famous, just like Him.

5

When I was younger, I used to tell my teachers that I had a baby brother at home. I told this story to everyone else, too. Later on I learned that this was called *lying*. But at the time, I thought it was just a story about a different kind of life. In this other life, I was not an only child. Everyone else I knew had brothers and sisters, so I thought it would make me feel better to make up a story about having a baby brother. Now that I'm older, I'm happy that my family is just me, my mom, and my dad.

I know that it's fine to be an only child. Because Jesus loves me, and someday I'm going to be famous, just like Him. You don't have to have brothers and sisters to be famous.

Let me tell you what it has been like for me at school. I have had a very hard time learning how to read. It was frustrating for me, because I am a great talker and I love to tell stories. It was strange being able to *tell* stories but not being able to read them. I needed a lot of help. Math was hard for me, too. I tried and tried, but I had so much trouble with it. I saw that the other kids around me were not having as much trouble, and sometimes it made me feel sad. I can read and do math much better now, but I remember how it felt not to be able to, even though I was trying my best.

I know that no matter what other people might say about me, God is proud of me when I try my best. Because Jesus loves me, and someday I'm going to be famous, just like Him. You don't have to be the best student in the world to be famous.

Sometimes the girls in other classes were mean to me and called me names. I used to try and sit with them at lunch, but some of them didn't want to sit with me. They said I was too fat and they laughed at me and teased me. I didn't like how they made me feel. I knew that what they did to me was wrong, but after this happened, I decided to exercise more and eat right. It really hurt my feelings when the girls teased me, but I still tried hard to take better care of myself.

I know that God wants me to do my best to stay healthy because it's good for me, not because it will help me make friends. Because Jesus loves me, and someday I'm going to be famous, just like Him. You don't need a million friends in school to be famous.

My last year at this school was the worst year of all. I was in the fifth grade. I was so mad that I was the only girl in my class. I was surrounded by a bunch of boys! How could I talk to them about girl things? I was too old to have a best friend who was a boy. I needed to have a best *girl* friend so we could talk and do things together. I felt so lonely. I couldn't wait for the school year to be over.

I know that having a very best friend in school would be a lot of fun, but it's not the most important thing in the world. Because Jesus loves me, and someday I'm going to be famous, just like Him. You don't need a best friend to be famous.

I had a teacher in my fifth grade class who didn't understand me. I didn't understand her either. I didn't know why she did and said mean things to me. Once at a Christmas party, I spent all afternoon making Christmas ornaments and talking about Jesus. I didn't know it was supposed to be called a "winter holiday party" and we weren't supposed to talk about Jesus like we do in church. When it was time to clean up, she told me to throw all my ornaments away in the trash! I didn't want to, so she did it herself. She said that decorations about Jesus didn't belong in school. Later I found out it was because she didn't even believe in God. I felt so sad, but part of me was very mad at her, too. On the school bus I cried all the way home.

I know that it's good to be a Christian everywhere I go, even if people don't understand me or treat me nicely because of the way I believe. Because Jesus loves me, and someday I'm going to be famous, just like Him. You don't need to be understood or treated nicely to be famous.

When school was almost over, another bad thing happened. I tried to join in with the other girls and play jump rope with them, but this same teacher told me I couldn't. She said I had something called a *disability*. I didn't even know what that was! I was sad and confused. I asked my mom, "What is a disability?" But she said not to worry about it. She was upset about what happened, but I wasn't exactly sure why. For a long time I didn't really know what the word meant, but then recently my mom told me I am autistic. I'm trying to learn more about autism.

I know that there is nothing wrong with trying to play with *all* the kids at school, even if someone else tells me I don't fit in. Because Jesus loves me, and someday I'm going to be famous, just like Him. Even if you are different, you can still be famous.

After the school year was over, I spent the summer thinking about what *famous* meant. I wondered what it would be like to be famous. I thought, maybe I could be famous like a princess! I could live in a castle and wear a fancy dress. I would be the smartest, prettiest, and richest girl in all the kingdom. I could have all the friends I wanted and play any games that I wanted. If I were a princess, nobody would ever dare throw out something I made with my own two hands.

But then I thought, *that's* not the same way Jesus was famous. If I was going to be famous someday just like Jesus, I needed to figure out what it was that made Him so famous.

So then I thought, maybe I could be famous like a movie star! When my new movies came out, I could walk on a big red carpet. Lots of people would take pictures of me everywhere I went, and I could be on the covers of magazines and newspapers. Everyone would think that I was very fancy because my clothes would be expensive, and my hair and makeup would be perfect all the time. I would be so rich that I could buy anything I wanted. I could live in a great big mansion, and I would not have to do anything except make movies.

But then I thought, *that's* not the same way Jesus was famous. If I was going to be famous someday just like Jesus, I needed to figure out what it was that made Him so famous.

Maybe I could be a famous opera singer! I could get up on stage and sing so loud and so strong that I wouldn't even need a microphone. Everyone would be amazed at how talented I was. I could sing in all different languages, and people would love me even if they didn't understand what I was singing. I could travel all over the world, wear beautiful costumes, and perform in the fanciest concert halls. I could be a *diva*! Being a diva is almost like being a princess. Divas feel very important because they are so talented.

But then I thought, *that's* not the same way Jesus was famous. If I was going to be famous someday just like Jesus, I needed to figure out what it was that made Him so famous.

That summer I saw the Olympics on TV. I heard the crowds cheering for all the athletes, and I noticed that everyone kept talking about the Olympics on all the TV stations. So I thought, maybe I could be an Olympic gymnast! I would jump and run and twirl. I would fly through the air as the crowds cheered: "Sara! Sara! Sara!" I would win a dozen gold medals and get to stand on a box with a wreath on my head. I would hold my hand over my heart, and the band would play The Star-Spangled Banner. What a great day that would be for me!

But then I thought, *that's* not the same way Jesus was famous. If I was going to be famous someday just like Jesus, I needed to figure out what it was that made Him so famous.

So I thought long and hard about why none of these jobs would make me famous the same way Jesus was. I thought, if I had any of these jobs, I would spend most of my time trying to get better and better at something. I would want people to clap and cheer for me when they saw me and all of my hard work. In each of these jobs, I would be a different kind of entertainer. Entertainers can be good people, because they can make people feel very happy inside. But this happiness lasts only for a little while. It does not change people's lives forever. That's not the way Jesus was. He was famous, but He was not an entertainer. What made Him famous then? I thought about this for a long time.

Finally I remembered what my parents had taught me! Jesus was famous for showing the world God's love. That's why Jesus died for us. He didn't care about being the richest, or the smartest, or the most important. He cared just about us and not Himself. So when He decided to die on the cross, He did it to show us how much God really loves us. He decided to let others tease and hurt Him so that we could be with Him in heaven forever. He took away our sins because He knew that people couldn't do this all by themselves. Even today, Jesus helps us do all kinds of things that we can't do all alone, no matter how hard we try. I wanted to be like that, too. I wanted to help others and show them God's love. At last I knew how I was going to be famous! So then I began to think about some things I could do when I grow up.

When I grow up I could help children who don't have any brothers or sisters, maybe even children who don't have any mothers and fathers, too. I could help people who feel like they are all alone in the world. I could tell them that maybe God allowed *me* to grow up as an only child so that He could show me how to help others who feel like they are all alone. I could tell them that once they know God they never have to feel lonely anymore. I could tell them that even when Jesus was left all alone right before He died, He still had His heavenly Father to pray to. I could teach them to pray to their heavenly Father.

Maybe someday I will be able to help children who tell me they are sad and lonely, because that's what Jesus would do if they told Him. That's the kind of thing that made Him famous.

When I grow up I could help children who are having trouble in school. I could help them learn to read and write and do math. I could tell them that maybe God allowed *me* to struggle in school at first so that I would know what it was like and how it felt. I could be a very special teacher to many students because I would be able to understand why they were having trouble learning. Maybe I could even open a special school and be the principal. I would tell my students that I just wanted them to enjoy learning and try their very best.

Maybe someday I will be able to help children who tell me they are having trouble in school, because that's what Jesus would do if they told Him. That's the kind of thing that made Him famous.

When I grow up I could help kids who are having trouble keeping their weight down. I would teach them how to exercise and eat the right kinds of foods. I would teach them that God made our bodies, and that He wants us to take good care of ourselves. That way we won't get sick and we will be able to enjoy the lives God has given us. I could explain that maybe God allowed *me* to struggle with my weight at first so that I could help others who are having the same problem. That way I could understand exactly how they feel. Maybe I could open up a fitness center for children where kids could come and learn about Jesus while getting healthy and fit. Maybe it would be the first fitness center like that in the whole world!

Maybe someday I will be able to help kids who tell me they want to take better care of their bodies, because that's what Jesus would do if they told Him. That's the kind of thing that made Him famous.

When I grow up I could ask God to give me a daughter. That way if some girls are mean to her, if she is the only girl in her class, if some teachers are mean to her, if she has trouble in school, or if she just feels lonely and has nobody else to turn to, *I* could be her best friend, just like my mom is *my* best friend. I would have a loving Christian husband, just like my dad. I would be happy with a family of three, just like mine. I could be famous, even if it was just to people in my family.

Maybe someday I will be a best friend to my daughter if she asked me to, because that's what Jesus would do if she asked Him. That's the kind of thing that made Him famous.

But even if for some reason I never get to do any of these jobs or be any of these things, I can *still* be famous, just like Jesus:

I can pray for people who are sad and lonely.

I can pray for people who feel unhealthy or sick.

I can pray for people with disabilities.

And I can even pray for my *enemies*, too. I can pray that God will teach them to treat *all* people with kindness and respect. I can pray for God to forgive all the people in my life who have ever been mean to me.

Because God forgave me, and He doesn't want to see unforgiveness in my heart. In God's eyes, I will be famous for praying for my enemies.

And you know what else? Now there's a *book* about me, just like there's a book about Jesus. Jesus shows us God's love every time we read the Bible. And every time you read this book about me, I can share some of God's love with you, too!

This is my true story. David is one of my friends from my old class. He is Lisa's son. Lisa wrote this book, and she is a good friend of mine. I visit Lisa a lot at her house. Lisa gave me the perfect name, Sara the Famous. I pray to Jesus every night. Whoever reads my story, I hope you will enjoy it. Thank you.

—Sara

Printed in the United States
By Bookmasters